I0119728

George M. (George Milbry) Gould

An autumn singer

George M. (George Milbry) Gould

An autumn singer

ISBN/EAN: 9783337374730

Printed in Europe, USA, Canada, Australia, Japan

Cover: Foto ©Thomas Meinert / pixelio.de

More available books at **www.hansebooks.com**

An Autumn Singer

By

George M. Gould, A.M., M.D.

Philadelphia

J. B. Lippincott Company

Mdcccxcvii

COPYRIGHT, 1896,

BY

GEORGE M. GOULD.

PRINTED BY J. B. LIPPINCOTT COMPANY, PHILADELPHIA, U.S.A.

Table of Contents

SONGS

7

AN AUTUMN SINGER

A BIT of sunshine, warmed by spring,
    A heart of song, a fluff of feather,
A wing put there, and here a wing,
    A breath blown in,—all kissed together
With sweet, low croon of half-heard words,—
This was the way Love made his birds!

A world of sunshine, wooed by spring,
    Breathed down on meadow, field, and wood,
A brooding sense in everything
    Of benediction soft and good
O'er ripening old and blithe new-comer,—
And this the way Love made his summer!

A wise, good bird who can't be mother
    The next best chooses, mightiest, metest,—
Close by her nest, some place or other,
    He sits and sings to her his sweetest,—

Sings all day long, and summer long,—
'Twas thus that Love made summer-song!

With nestlings flown flew confidence,
    And then he felt how poor his singing—
To silence shamed, and penitence;
    Ah! no! The dear one said, close winging,
Your song my comfort was, defence!
And thus Love brought song's recompense!

All through the spring, the summer through,
    Dear birds, you filled and thrilled the air
With song that only God and you
    Could make together, each his share
Of utter best and sweetest bringing,—
Thus Love filled all his world with singing!

And then when summer's work was done
    And Love no longer needed you,
A death-like silence fell, till one,
    Aggrieving, wondered what to do
With life when all its good had left,—
Such was the world of love bereft.

When autumn came, lone here, far there,
  Were heard want's tremulous notes, and wrong's
Weak rilling tones of tuneless air,—
  Such pale, pathetic, songless songs
To silence melting faint above!—
Thus Love mocked singing without love!

When all the air was music, one,
  Untaught of song, unskilled in tune,
Sat silent until, startling, run
  And stirred Life's great migration rune,—
Then burst and gushed the long-stored flow,—
An autumn-singer's want and woe!

O Love! knit well our wings, and fill
  To brimming all our hearts with song;
Migration past, assure shall thrill
  New spring, new life, atoning, strong!
Ah! Shall we find new world above?
And thee, thee, Love? O Love! O Love!

THE SONNET

THE sonnet is a photograph of one
    Rich evanescent moment of Life's face,
    Whose beauty subtly to a differing grace
Each instant glides, o'er which fleet-footed run,
Like shine and shadow alternate of sun
    'Cross goldening corn-fields, the elusive chase
    Of smiles and tears, and joys and sorrows race,
Till shower and shine have end and day is done.

A photograph of soul by spirit light
    Flashed in the world's impermanence,—
        The glance that passes and the phase that
            flies,—
Revealing man, unfrightened by time's flight,
    With faith and mind transcending doubt and
        sense,
    A heart that cries, *I live*, to heart that dies.

NIGHT-MYSTERIES

THE midnight moon at sky-edge pauses, swings,
  To view her world with pale wan darkness
    bright.
The silence deepens; quivers unseen light,
And half-heard, hover whirring wondrous wings;
The sighs and breaths of mystic bodiless things
  Against the air-wove walls of being smite,
  While broods the hush and mystery of the
    night,
Soft pressing on the spirit's inner springs.

Are we, are we, of night, and life, and time,
  Awaiting birth-hour? Do we subtly feel,
    Enwombed and mothered of Eternity,
Her pulsing heart-beats rippling through us
    rhyme?
  Among our dreams thy love's low crooning
    steal,
  Dear Mother, thou, who yearnest till we be?

REJECTED

Twin mountain pools, her eyes, filled from far
       springs,
  Hid in cool, sweet, and quiet wood, with shade
  Of bordering mosses, and with palisade
Of flowers. Even now I hear the bird that sings
His gush of wildwood song that limpid rings,—
  And hearing that rapt, holy serenade
  Stills Silence all the lisping leaves, and glade,
And holds her heart, while day to nightfall wings.

Life's question once I asked those mysteried eyes
  Of gaze impersonal and unabashed;
    And peering down their depths I saw there—
    God,
Who looked at me with pitying love, o'erwise,
  As she referred my wish to Him: quick flashed
  Responsive back His stern dissenting nod.

A VISION OF PEACE AND REST

As hurled by Titan-wrath roars on the train,
    And swift past windows whirl hot gleams of
        things
    Which tire the wearied monotone that sings
The Soul, life's journey through. Startled, I
    strain
To see far under noble trees, where reign
    Deep sunflecked shades, cool silences, and
        springs,
    Sweet mystic murmuring leaves and brooks and
        wings,—
A glance of Paradise with eyes of Pain.

As once, in rush of doubt and heart-distress,
    I saw Eternal Peace and Rest supreme!
      One instant let my aching eyes explore
The cool, green, silent depths that hush and bless,
    Where God's dreams shimmer, fall asleep, and
        dream,—
      I heard their muffled pulses, then—no more!

BANISHED

In world awaked the soul looks out along
  The coming years,—halts sorrow-hushed, and
    thrilled;
  The eyes far-seeing, fear and wonder-filled,
Catch hint of coming love, or waiting wrong,
Perhaps of both combined, in one life-long
  Desire that dies not, and cannot be stilled,
  Or hope that lives not, yet cannot be killed,
By Life more weak than Death, than Death more
    strong.

Then backward runs the lost world-fleeing child
  Along the road that inward leads to God,
    Falls at the awful gates, implores, and clings,
Between his stifled sobs rains kisses wild
  On bolts, with tears and fondlings begs each rod
  Of the relentless, silent, iron things.

HER LAUGH

I'm sure God's favorite angels laugh just so,—
Or, when she goes to heaven, she'll teach them
to!
Perhaps a memory 'tis of their adieu
When she came thence to us! At first a slow,
Soft gurgle in the heart of gladness low
An instant bubbles, then quick gushes through
The sweetest throat, to break in air and strew
The limpid music of joy's overflow.
And then half frightened, down and back she
calls
The truant notes escaped, which flash and go
Home to her heart with little lisp and coo
Of love's delight, and little gasps and falls!—
I'm sure His dearest angels laugh just so,
Or that when she goes there, they'll learn
how to!

THE WORLD'S ORCHESTRA

ALL history seems as if the players tried
    Their instruments, the keys and strings ran o'er,
    Essaying modulation, bar of score,
Until with each they should be satisfied,
While waiting and expectant they abide
    A dominant will that shall to all restore
    The unity and purpose planned before,
And discords melt to music glorified.

O Love! Of cosmic orchestra and choir
    The leader, master, thou awaited long,
      Come seize our wills, command to harmony
The notes discordant of our life's desire!
    Make nations sing the antiphonal song
      Of Peace, the world play thy grand sym-
      phony!

THE SOUL'S MASQUE

THE soul is like the man in visored steel
   Whose face by strange mysterious decree
   He dare reveal to none, none live and see.
The body is the masque whose folds conceal,
More absolute than iron's locked anneal,
   Soul-prisoner hid within.   Whate'er the plea,
   Self's secret deep is kept more utterly
Than were it doom of death should we reveal.

And hence our piteous, awful loneliness!
   Alone we live and die, and cannot tell
      The truth although the secret kill; unshown
Soul's face to dearest friend!   More merciless,
   Fate makes us mysteries to ourselves—in cell
      Of flesh unknown of all, by self unknown!

UNREST

THE mountain spring o'erruns to rivulet,
    The brook to river, hurrying, onward goes,
    Yearns river toward the sea, and as it flows
Dreams ending there of all life's want and fret.
But vainly seeks the ocean to forget!
    Pain's note, subdominant of woes,
    Moans ever in its heart's adagios,
Remorseless, sleepless, as divine regret.

So run our lives and doings, pitiless,
    To infinite ocean of humanity;
    But still at heart of nation, world, we see
Insatisfaction's hunger, soul's distress,
    To tide of passion, storm of battle, roll,
    While prays for peace and rest the warring
        soul.

AN "MUTTER ERDA"

For this a million years the world-soul wrought;
   And history strained the wedding not to miss,
   When Earth, the bride, all hungry for the kiss,
Should proffer lips, lift face, and be upcaught
In God's down-stooping love. In world is not
   So great, so pure, so sweet a thing as this :—
   The darling child enthroned in mother-bliss,
And ecstasy of lambent love and thought.

A silent song of victory is her smile;
   Her eyes past yours look into God's own eyes;
     'Tis Love's soft hands that push each pulse-
      beat fine
From mother-heart into the girl-face, while
   The baby-sphinx propounds Life's riddle wise
     Which makes the answerer, as these two,
      divine.

DE NOVO

How poor I was! And only yesterday!
  I had no heart great things to do or dare.
  My faiths or hopes were shadowed or were fair
As drifted, or did not, across my May
Of life, the clouds of chance their aimless way.
  And then your eyes blazed into mine a share
  Of Love's own soul, your lips!—O rich and rare
Is now the air I breathe, the life I play!

Ah, Love, Love, Love! Thy miracle is new
  However old it be; thy sweet more sweet
Than ever other knew. Truth now is true,
  And Beauty beautiful. Dear face and feet,
Turn not henceforth away from me! Dear hands,
Draw closer evermore the holy bands!

THE LIFE THAT NOW IS

For intellect that loves, and heart that knows,
  All other faith is naught except it be
  This faith, this knowledge, of the life we see
And are. Why not enough? Strong, sweet it
      grows,
With infinite plenitude ; all pains and woes
  Of matter's incarnation-mystery
  Weigh not a perfumed petal falling free
From this divinely splendid cosmic rose,—
Our one world-blossom from God's own rose-tree
  Abloom in all the gardened fields of space,—
    Whose flower dies not though fall its leaves
      to death.
Its leaves are souls.   The flower eternally
  Draws truth and beauty from the Gardener's
      face,
    And Love, its fragrance, is His very breath.

LIFE'S PHILOSOPHY

With ever-varying color, mystic, strange,
   Two rainbowed streams of light from far-off
      skies
   Unroll into our dark, and flash as with the dyes
Of day and night, of heaven and hell, they change,
And weave in nearer-greeting, recognizing range.
   And then they interweave and blend, while rise
   And flood the earth, and fill all seeing eyes,
The incarnate wonders of life's interchange.

Our world is fusion of the single lights
   Of me and thee in marriage-death divine,
   And beauty is God's benediction-sign;
Our Freedom is forgetfulness of rights,
   The Truth is our forgetfulness of wrong,
   And Happiness is Love's own weaving-song.

THE LOVE OF GOD

WHAT mean we when we say we must love God?
    Contentment with thought-fashions, creeds?
    Atonement idle for our idle deeds?
If love we have we pass beneath His rod,
And tread the lonely ways His feet have trod;
    We heal and bind the wounded heart that
        bleeds,
    With life and love fill full the heart that needs,
Till breaks to spring our world, as flowers from
    sod.

How tireless does He work by day and night,
    To loose the bonds of Fate and set Love free!
He gladness sheds, as does the sun its light,
    On child and bird and flower.   What artist He!
In all His work laughs Beauty's holy, bright,
    Immortalizing *Benedicite*.

3   25

AWAIT THE BLOWING OF THE ROSE

Our childish science plucks the budding rose
  Of knowledge, pulls its leaves apart to spy
  What hidden secret at its heart may lie.
We find a wondrous living flower that glows,
Within hid leaf enfolding leaf, and grows
  New mysteries forever. Then we cry
  With pain of baffled hope, or worse, deny
The beauty, life, the flower itself, that blows.

But why not wait the natural day of bloom
  Of Evolution's Rose divine? Because
    It takes a million years, and waits death's
      hour?
But listen! Hear God laugh at time and doom!
  He bids you by His courier loves and laws
  Come see the Universe about to flower.

THE SCEPTIC'S CONSOLATION

WHAT then abides in all this mystic dance
　　Of seeming real and unreal, me, not me?
　　Our firmest faiths, the surest truths, we see
Illusive fade,—our sole inheritance
The accident of fate, or fate of chance.
　　The eye creates the thing it sees, yet we
　　Slow learn that eye and subjectivity
Are woof of dream and warp of circumstance.

The dream abides! The law and fact of change!
　　The surety too that woven warp and woof
　　　Has loveliness for infinite delight.
Know all mutation's laws, let range
　　The eye their glories o'er,—enough the proof
　　　Of world perdurable, in beauty dight.

REALITY

THE beauty of the wondrous world and sky,
  Their color, light, the bitter and the sweet
  Of subtile sense, the harmonies that greet
The ear, or jars that hurt,—all seem to lie
Without. But only seem; for they by ear and
    eye
  Are made,—or powers that senses make and
    mete;
  From crude material hint or quiver fleet
The mind creates the world we deify.

Ah, Truth and Love! Fear ices all my heart,
  To think ye too may be phantasmic plays,
    Born of our wants, Illusion's aureole!—
But then no anodyne could reach our smart,
  And threadless evermore the infinite maze,
    Were not reality enthroned in soul.

IMMORTALITY

You hunger for eternal life, and fain
  Through death would bear the group of vani-
    ties,
  Of weakness, wants, and waste inanities,
You fondly cherish as yourself. How vain !
Pray, rather, for kind death to end your pain,
  Your love of self, of pleasure, and of ease;
  Not Him, not Him, your worthless gift may
    please,—
Must lose one's life, I've heard, true life to gain.
It were malignant, not beneficent,
  Our starveling wants and weakness to endow
  With awful doom of perpetuity.
Just wisdom and true goodness both consent
  Will certain find God there who finds Him now.
  Who not immortal is, will never be.

FOUR FAILURES [1]

THE eaglets oft missed aim and fish, but won
    Sometimes, and screaming bore aloft their prey
    To stuff their maws—the old accustomed way.
One failed, learned well miscalculation none
Dare be when life is staked in hazards run ;
    His talons could not leave, his wings not sway
    The victim, soon the victor of the fray,
Which dragged him living, dead, till life was done.

The story's old with men who devil's game
    Of "politics" or "business" play 'gainst soul ;
Most lose ; some win their pitiable wealth or fame,
    But one I saw, endowed for nobler goal,
Swoop conscious down, find talons locked in shame,
    And he of beast tormented, carcass-troll.

THE MEN OF MARS

O Martian men, my mind is tired with strain
   And eager fancy to catch hint what you
   May be, how act, of what you think, as through
The awful depths of space I peer, till fain
To you I'd leap across the ethereal main.
   Ah, if what you know, we but surely knew!
   Have you found God? Are you just, pure, and
      true?
What is your reading of life's riddle, what your
      pain?

With all our doubts and wonderings this we
      find :—
You are what we shall yet become when mind
   Shall conquer sense, and from white pole to
      pole,
   The streams of universal peace shall roll.
We wait, content to know, however far,
Life's heart and love's beat warm in far-off star.

THE MATTERHORN

Thy bases rooted in the immobile deep
  Of earth, with giant buttresses of rock,
  Scorn Titan's blow, heed not the earthquake's
    shock.
Lured on, the eyes climb up the dizzying steep
To rest upon the beetling heights that keep
  Eternal watch above the world, and mock
  The littleness of man.   About thee flock
Thy tribute-mountains.   Silence sinks to sleep.

'Twas said who reads life's riddle not aright
  Quick finds himself bereft of life's own breath.
    Dost thou, O Sphinx of Mountains, mitigate
Our doom, and from us hold by mastering might
  The eternal eyes whose awful glance is death?
    Thy gaze meets full the gorgon-stare of Fate.

INDEPENDENCE

THE world loves honor only in dead men,
   And crowns them as its kings at last when they
   Are past delight of duty, joy of day;
In life it gives success to servant when
Good tool he's been of end ignoble,—then,
   The dupe dismisses on Oblivion's way.
   Who dares such master scorn and disobey
Must seek reward beyond all earthly ken.

But fears no revolution who is king
   Of self, sole subject true,—more undesired,—
      Whose kingdom's limits touch nor sea nor
      shore.
No fame or power that might the great world
      bring
Is worth the proud content and joy inspired
   By his own soul's *Well done!* What needs
   he more?

AGE

IT is so long between the thought and doing,
  So weary long between the deed and crown,
  That runs the fount of Youth to Age slow down,
And bubbles low, sleep only half subduing.
How strange now seems our ardent young pursu-
      ing,
  So worthless is the o'er-belate renown,
  So harmless is stern Disapproval's frown,
And charmless the long-wooed now come a-woo-
      ing.

'Tis Death that waits us when desire runs low;
  Then sad we smile at youth's delusions sweet,
And, weary, long eternal sleep to know;—
  'Tis Death, whom once we feared and shrank to
      meet,
  Whom now we trust, and reach forth hand to
      greet;
He loving draws the hand: we rise to go.

THE OCEAN²

I.

As it once was, so it again shall be!

　As it once was! Ah, then o'er world and
　　'round

　No line of shore rose up to mock, no bound,

No rock's or mount's impertinence; free, free

Of limit and of will, we mighty three

　　Then ruled the universe alone; no sound

　　There was except 'round all the world the sound

Of my wild waves in wild hoarse whirr of glee.

We mighty three! The children of old Fate,

Who died of grief, and willed eternal hate

　　To his presumptuous heirs, star-crownèd Night,

　　And Day, who took from him his sun and light,

And me, who seized the world, and over these,

His Titans and his mountains, spread my seas!

How little dreamed or recked I of their hate,
   Those cumbrous minions of my father's sway,
   In caverns prisoned, hid from night and day;
Their groans I heard not, thought not of their state,
Their plottings, or their just or unjust fate.
   Enough for me the swift and splendid play
   Of wind with wave, of sun with wave and spray,
The swell and sweep of tide importunate.

I sported with the lightning, and the stroke
   Of thunder on my face, the lash of storm,
Caresses were that me from slumbering woke
   To answer elemental boasts with roar enorme
Of laughter, till earth's caves and deeps profound
Reverberant rocked with muffled boom of sound.

They heard the laughter, felt derision's sting;
  Through all the caverns of their gaols and hearts
  Pierced sharp the shame,—till shame o'ergoaded
      starts
And roars of hate and vengefulness outring.
Defies not power, nor fate, nor anything,
  Despair made desperate; it strength imparts
  To weakness, giants makes to gods, gives arts
Unto the dull,—to power an end may bring!

Through all their prisons rang the awful word;
  One mind of hell in myriad limbs was hurled;
Firm-braced they strained, until afar was heard
  The ominous splintering of the riving world.
Then thunder filled and deafened all the air,—
And mountain-mounting Titans mocked despair.

When circumstance o'errules and fate denies,
   When unto will is set unconquerable will,
   Then sinks the great mind in itself until
By subtle means remote it wins allies
Which work to hidden end that none descries.
   At last, the loyalty of things to skill,
   The world await for all-resolved will
Give victory to the enemy of lies.

Heaped continents of rock based deep in earth,
   Star-neighboring mountains, miles on miles of
      shore,—
These all are doomed! Sport of my mighty mirth
   They yet shall be; high over them and o'er
I yet shall ride as once I rode when free
Was given light to Day, night Night, my world to
      me!

Were loyal, brother Day, and sister Night;
 They swore me help, and we true royal three
 Swore as it once was it again shall be.
We set great tasks to all our servants: light
With darkness alternates; fire and frost unite
 To melt and burst and crumble down to me
 All haughty heights, till sunk beneath my sea,
Blown waves shall chase and laugh above them
   white.

There is no granite bulwark anywhere
 That shows not deep the markings of my teeth;
'Gainst every shore-line wash, and waste, and wear
 My tireless waves, and leave the frothing wreath
Of their mad lips, thus fresh reiterate
Eternal proofs of my eternal hate.

Day's chiefs, the sun and winds, are noble
    friends;
  They take my breath and carry it in cloud;
  The lands and mounts as with a shroud
Are covered, drenched; each loyal drop descends
To clutch its mite of earth, and hurrying blends
    With others into brooks, and brooks to rivers
    crowd,
  To roll relentless down the pride o'erproud
Till world of land in world of water ends.

Most fine shall all be ground! I pulverize
  And spread so wide that neither force nor fire
May rouse to union death that dies and lies
  So deep, and far, and fine, none may conspire;
In scorn I fling the unground pebbles back
To show earth's children my design and wrack!

Relentless as fate,
Forgetless as hate,
    Resistless as time,
My work shall go on, and go on ;
    All things I dissolve,
    To me all devolve ;
        Deep down in my slime
I bury them all, all, anon.

    The glacier is mine,
    The snow is my sign,
        Delay is not rest ;
Each shows me or early or late,
    Outworking command,
    Downfall of the land,
        The end of the quest,
The law and my reign vindicate.

My avalanche knells,
My earthquake foretells,
    My cyclone unchains
The doom ever nearing and dire;
    The tide and the flood
    Are pulses of blood
        In my eager veins,—
The ardors of my fierce desire.

    Each day they sink lower,
    Each day it runs slower,—
        These mountains, that life;
Submerged past all rising or breath,
    Soon lie land and shore
    'Neath waves evermore,
        Where end want and strife,
Where Time waits and wishes for death.

My lakes to me call,

Fain, fain would they fall,

Again with me rest,

Or eager fulfil water's work;

They soon shall be freed,

Released to their deed,

Recrown Dispossessed,—

O'er land and its parasites bask.

Dissolve every island,

Eat lowland and highland,

O Rain, Storm, and Flood,—

Again to me bear the proud earth!

Sun, burn them with fire!

Night, freeze them entire!

Streams, bring them as mud,

For burial fitting their worth!

Relentless as fate,

Forgetless as hate,

Resistless as time,

My work shall go on, and go on;

All things I dissolve,

To me all devolve;

Deep down in my slime

I bury them all, all, anon.

The giants long are dead; these too shall die,
  Their starveling heirs, called men, who eat and sin
  A dreary round of days before they win
The death they seek and fear with dread and lie.
A brief respite I give ere I deny
  Them food and foothold at their earthly inn,—
  I scorn to kill; I take my own; no kin
Are these of mine,—let them their fathers cry!

Content while sure the fateful centuries fall
  I wait, enjoy my victory every hour,
    As grain by grain I melt their mountains
    down,
Gnaw hills away, through ruined valleys brawl,
  With spoil of conquered continents and power,
    While hiss my storms, and driven waters
    drown.

At last shall flash the glitter and the glance
  Of lambent sunshine luminant and swift,
  Among my limpid waves, the sheen and shift
Of mystic moon-path shimmer dance,
Across the whole pure landless world's expanse.
  Then boreal streamers high shall dart and lift
  Their signals from white snow and pole-ice drift
To tell of peace and of deliverance.

Her covering, then, moon-wove and star-im-
      pearled,
  Will spread the slumber-bringing, soft, sweet
      Night,
Till, 'round and 'round the wondrous water-world,
  Day's sun shall chase the fleeing morning's
      flight.
And then! Eternal, lifeless, deathless, free,
Shall rule the glad, wide world we mighty three!

ABSENCE

O soft, insistent breeze that homeward yearns,
Each leaflet here atremble is and turns
    To fly with thee; its pulses passionate stir,
    And fond it whispers low, Take me to her!

        Go, go, and kiss her hair,
            Winds that run and woo;
        Kiss her eyes, wonder-fair,
            Say her lover's true!

O homing wind, o'er all the far way glide,
And tell who waits her at the window-side,
    The curtain fluttering,—beg her open free
    The blinds, her arms, her heart, to us—to me!

        Blow, blow, and stronger blow,
            Wind from out the south;
        Kiss her eyes, and, below—
            Tenderly—her mouth!

THE SECRET

THE Breeze whispered it to the Cloud,
   Half aloud;
The Clouds told it all to the Moon,
   Just as soon;
The Moon hid it not from her Star,
   High and far;
The Stars could not help telling Night,
   Love's delight;
At sunrise the Night told the Day—
   Blushed deep they!

So every one knew it but one,
   And she was too happy to care,
Perhaps with her love so undone,
   Or in her proud beauty too fair.

In some way, far south, got the birds
      Mystic words,
And straight started northward to see,
      In great glee;
Dropped snatches and hints of the song
      All along;
And when they arrived, found it true,—
      Same as you!—
That Spring had said " Yes," to her June,
      Married soon!

A sweet tripled, low-rippled word,
   The secret that everywhere purled;
Lips waiting, the bliss—no one heard!
   But quivered with rapture the world!

LOVE'S DAY

BEFORE the day begun
Through flushing East forerun
A trembling sense of sun,
And yearning to be won,—
Confession's sweet confused delight
Of scarlet deep transfusing white,
   Till bloomed the earth undone,
   To morning flowered like none,
And blossomed day from bud of night.

   Then day wrought on to noon,
   And hope waned all too soon
   To fall of afternoon,
   To sunset's dream and swoon,—
Till starts aroused the tear-filled eye
And hears tired heart the long-hid sigh,
   That love's and life's great tune
   Has softened down to croon
Of life and love that sleep and lie.

A SONG IN THE NIGHT

I DREAMED of thee deep in the night star-filled,
  And of my wrong;
Heard clear a call I thought was thine, that thrilled
  My soul along,—
And woke to find the cry a passion-filled
  Lone lark's night-song.

From night, O love, of thy denial go
  My yearnings strong,
In night-song of desire and heart-o'erflow
  Of night o'erlong,—
Ah, will it waken thee from dream, and, lo!
  Find answer-song?

BEND, BEND LOWER, LOVE

BEND, bend lower, love,
  Bend thy face to mine!
Raise, raise higher, love,
  Raise my face to thine!
Purse my waiting lips
With thy finger-tips,—
  Kiss me long!

Deep, deep, deeper, love,
  Deep within my eyes,
See, see, see, my love,
  How my whole soul dies
If thou do not bring me
Home to thee and sing me
  As thy song.

THE UNKNOWN LOVE

As April longing burns toward perfect June,
  As waits the bud for its sweet flowering time,
Or as a straying note for its lost tune,—
  So yearns my soul, O dear unknown, for thine.

To thee I send my greeting, unknown love!
  O'er years and miles, where'er, whoe'er thou
    art,—
I send it forth to search like an ark-dove,
  Ah, shall it find a haven for my heart?

Then haste thy coming, thou my unseen love!
  For like a spirit from the flesh set free,
That errant, hoping, seeks the gates above,
  So seek I rest and peace,—a heaven in thee!

SONG

O SING, my heart, as blithe wood-bird,
   From heart o'errunning, sing!
Although forgotten be the word,
The melody will still be heard,
   For song's the only thing!

O wing, my heart, as wings the bird,
   Me to my sweetheart bring!
She will not say a single word,
But " I love you" will plain be heard,
   For love's the only thing!

JOY AND CARE

THE little mother's work at last was done,—
      Their wings were strong,
      Their hearts with song
Were filled, and sun, and summer; Love had won
The sweet, glad race with Time, in spring begun.

And then she sang to Care, at window high,
      Her farewell song,—
      Good-bye, and long,
Dear neighbor Care, Good-bye, good-bye, good-
    bye!
Afar I must with flying summer fly.

But why have you no mate to call and take
      You to the South?
      No baby-mouth
To fill and kiss? Why does my singing make
You cry as if your breaking heart would break?

THE HAPPY PLOUGHMAN

BREAKFAST was a daisy!—
    Gee up, Ben, gee!—
Sue will drive me crazy!—
    Get up there, Lee!—
Crazy with her smiles and ways,
With her cakes and jams and plays;
My, how short these days the days!—
    Wake up there, gee!

Who can plough a furrow—
    Ho, haw, now, Ben!—
Straighter or more thorough?—
    Get along, then!
Baby—you can see him grow!
What a little cuss to crow!
I'm the luckiest dog I know,—
    Jog along, men!

JEALOUS

Countless lovers kneel before you,
  Beg you choose;
All devoted, all adore you,
  Claim their dues;
Whisper cloud and wind from o'er you
  Not refuse;
E'en the stars, I think, implore you
  Interviews.

Jealous I of all and fearing
  Bird and flower;
Envious of all endearing
  You them shower;
Tired of always overhearing
  Of their power,
While you give no hint of cheering
  My lone hour.

Mad I'd rather be or gay with
      Pets that crawl;
Dog would be or bird you play with,
      Come at call;
Eyes, indeed, that me you slay with,
      Such your thrall!
Far more lips that you say nay with,
      Nay to all!

LIFE

Life is a woman who is to us sweet
If we so will it, and lay at her feet
Heart's adoration and loyalty sure,
Hiding command under guise most demure.

Life was my sweetheart, capricious but true,
While I was true to her, bore with her too,
When she was unjust, or wayward or cold—
Soon she came round again same as of old.

Life is my wife now, 'tis better that way;
Fate's hard to fight against, harder to play;
Coquetry's over, love's game is for life,—
If you'd be happy make sweetheart your wife!

SURELY LOVE IS IN THE AIR

Surely love is in the air,
  In the wind, or shine of sun !
Faint before me everywhere,
Soft and subtle, fond and fair,
  Tender eyes elude and run,—
Surely love is in the air !

Murmuring breezes hint caress ;
  Bird-songs waken wants within,—
Wants to hungers grow, distress ;
Tears will come and tears confess
  Love's old wayward wondrous sin,
Conquering all my willingness.

THE WEDDING

JUNE sends to his longed-for bride,
    Budding little May,
Compliments that waken pride,
Askings she " can ne'er abide,"—
    But she'll kiss her "nay."

Hear him call, then listening, wait,
    (Answer, answer, dear!)
Tenderest love he sends his mate;
Spring kneels to congratulate,
    "Wed him!" murmurs clear.

As the shine-flecks fondly chase
    Shadows over hill,
So her smiles and blushes race,
Sweet across the sweetest face,
    Full her pulses fill.

" Marry, marry !" sing the birds,
　　" All the earth's in tune !"
Winds and woods whirr eager words,—
May with flowers and garlands girds,—
　　May has married June !

SEASONS

'Twas long ago my spring
Passed summer on the wing,
And heard the autumn sing
The soft sad preluding
Of wintering months and days that sere,
Of song that hears song disappear,
While tears fill eyes and bring
Far memory of spring,
Faint scents of blighted flowers and year.

So love, long, long ago,
Broke from the springtime glow,
To autumn ripened slow,
Till came the winter's snow—
White mocker of that early gush
When reckless broke the wild sweet rush,
The ecstasy of woe
And life and love. Now, lo!
Age whispers both her silent, Hush!

JUNE

As soft as silence is the noon ;
   The leaves of every tree are stilled ;
The trees are full of love, and swoon
   To joyous sleep, with dreams fulfilled,
While high and faint the half-heard croon
   And lullaby of day, distilled
To monotone of ending tune,
   Drops softly down to dream, unthrilled
Of aught except the bliss and boon
   Of Heaven that broods, and God who willed
That Earth beloved should be of June.

USE AND BEAUTY

A LITTLE alien thing, a humble blade,
  Sprang up among the corn,
Which mocked in haughty pride and hid in shade
  A weed so lowly born ;
But Day and Night and Love a compact made,—
  It blossomed as the morn.

The winds blew wide apart the envious grain
  So sun could come to it;
From many lovers fond on hill and plain
  The bees with offerings flit ;—
And in the reaper's heart God whispered fain
  Its beauty's benefit.

ACTION[3]

Oh, sing the song of life with deeds!
  Their silent music richer is
  Than chorals, poems, symphonies,—
And all the world that music heeds.

When dies the singer, ends the song;
  When is no reading, then is none
  To tell of love, or lost, or won;
Even brass and marble teach time's wrong.

Not all the universe could hold
  World's wishings from the world effaced;
  Far better gold with stamp debased
Than in earth's depths ungathered gold.

Belief to feeling quick transform;
  Turn feeling to volition bold;
  Crowd life into the matter-mould,
Till all the earth with life is warm.

Let players play with words and thought,
 Do thou the deed, its telling shun ;
 Not God Himself undoes what's done ;
Is potter by the pot forgot ?

Fling forth your act then into fact,—
 And reckless of all consequence ;
 One moment or a million hence
Who can foresee what will react ?

The rule of law he only rules,
 Breaks in between cause and effect,
 Who can his deed, himself inject
As cause of cause, effects his tools.

The ethic-books of destiny grant
 The pride of god to him who bears
 Prolific child; with scorn it glares
At sterile and at dilettant.

They who strong life, great deed and fact
 In texture of the world-stuff weave,
 Death cannot harm them nor aggrieve :
They are immortal by their act.

Who life in statues incarnate,
  Who with real blood, real flesh-tints, draw,
  Who make religion into law,—
Forge freedom-links in chain of fate.

CONTEMPLATION[4]

SING not the song of life with deeds!
   Their music more discordant is
   Than chorals, poems, symphonies,
Which finer ear attunèd heeds.

When singer dies, ends not the song,
   But lives to tell a world to come
   Of love and truth the added sum;
The spirit laughs at all time's wrong.

Not all the universe could hold
   World's evil deeds from world effaced;
   Far worse the gold with stamp debased
Than in earth's depths the virgin gold.

With passion rend not reason's peace,
   Wreck feeling not on doing's rocks;
   Who mind in matter thoughtless locks
Imprisons her beyond release.

The wise contented are with thought,
    And boasting pride of action shun;
    Not God Himself undoes what's done;
Unbeauteous work is not unwrought.

Guard then to fling your will to fact,
    Like fool unrecking consequence;
    One moment or a million hence,
The thoughtless deed will full react.

The rule of law he only rules
    Who knows between cause and effect
    No thing can God or man inject,—
To break the sequence teach no schools.

The ethic-book of destiny showers
    Its curses on the man who bears
    Impotent children as the heirs
Of ill,—with sin the sinner dowers.

Who keep from matter's rule their life
    Serene and pure,—their souls are free
    From death and all world-mastery,
Untouched by time's ignoble strife.

Who lighten woe with song and art,
Who heal our wounds, not make them bleed,
Who lessen lust and ruth of deed,—
Uncoil Fate's chain from Freedom's heart.

APHORISMS

Our fate goes with us where we go;
 However fast or far
 We follow fondly star,
No nearer, warmer, is its glow.

Fear not the recompense of hell;
 Of heaven expect no gain;
 Atonement seeks in vain
Who does not in atonement dwell.

Not there or then our heaven awaits,
 But deep behind our eyes,
 Inferno, Paradise,
Our doom or blessing now creates.

The good of money is the gaining,
 The good of knowledge, seeking,
 Engagement and bespeaking
Refuses joy,—will no constraining.

Forever by your side is beauty
    And happiness if you
    Turn never them to view,—
Eyes forward fixed alone on duty.

The singer's guerdon is the song,—
    Because joy wills it so;
    The heart's glad overflow
Makes pain forgotten, right of wrong.

True lovers lovers are of love,
    More than of *him* or *her;*
    They god to priest prefer,
And rate the wine the cup above.

For life is life's reward and fee;
    The sum of good outweighs
    The evil of her days,
Or then, or now, or time to be.

And life is life's full frank excuse;
    If we've not happy been,
    We've loved our secret sin
More than the gift God gave for use.

6

THE OPEN SECRET

Conceal not your evil, my brother;
    'Tis writ in your face,
    Each glance shows its trace,
    Each word speaks disgrace :
Oh, hide not your sin from another !

There's ever a subtler than you
    Who knows your deep thought,
    Your plot, counterplot,
    Your would-be forgot,
And all you may think or may do.

Eyes you see not still see you ;
    Detectives are tracking,
    No use turn or tacking ;
    No cue or clew lacking,
Your " case " shall stand clear to all view.

You cannot deceive the All-wise,
    Who fixes in flesh,
    In bone and brain-mesh,
    Fate's seal and stamp fresh
On thought, wish, or will, as they rise.

EARTHLY IMMORTALITY

WE victims or of sin or ill's mischance
   Who do not forge our lives in Destiny's chain,
   Who choose to end the wondrous woven strain
That through a million years has wrought ad-
     vance,—
   Atoning recompense may hope in vain.

Too long in blinded self-delusion we
   Have mocked the living Deity of Deeds
   With empty words, philosophies, and creeds,
With eyes that looked but still that did not see,—
   While life's great work proceeded and proceeds.

What God is there in world of peace and strife,
   What proof of intellect, of love, or good,
   What show of kindness, or of fatherhood,

Except the living, laboring God of Life
  Whose will and worship we ignored, withstood?

In every blade of grass Himself He brings
  To light; of plant or tree the pure white blood
  He fashions, draws it to the preformed bud,
To flowering pushes buds, wherefrom well springs
  Of beauty and of sweet in perfumed flood.

How perfect is His workmanship in horns,
  Fangs, teeth, and stings, in hands, and feet, and
    wings!
  Through throats of His dear birds His gladness
    sings;
Despair of artist, what His art adorns!
  Our science is relearning His known things!

His deputies He has appointed us
  To use the finished products of His skill;
  And all the wrong of all the world's sad ill
Is our misuse of power,—His overplus
  Of pain to heal self-hurts of our self-will.

As best He can He heals, but scars are—scars;
  And what is broken, soiled, and worn is not
  So strong and pure again as what has caught
Its goodness fresh from Him; His avatars
  Are childhood, youth, and their ideals untaught.

For our perverted fancy, craving, He
  Recks not, but plain His work the lesson shows
  That only incarnation-sweets and woes
Insure the gift of immortality;—
  On egotists such gifts He scarce bestows!

Stand therefore on the bank, O childless one,
  And watch the stream of life glide by
  To wondrous lands you may not see, that lie
In future world, beneath a warmer sun
  That rises now, and shines from bluer sky.

Failed, failed, have you, disguise it as you will!
  Not even He, the great Forgiver, can
  Your sin forgive. He must outwork the plan!
Play out your idle day, its evening fill
  With wasted hours, as you its morn began.

The birds more loyal are than you, they fly
    With song and love full-filled, o'er continents,
    Obeying that divinely-whispered subtle sense
Which disobeyed, too late find you and I
    Gives all the wrong of laboring life's expense.

'Tis easy making our small virtues great,
    To magnify our little fact of worth
    Till hid all duty, even the whole wide earth;
Too exquisite were we, forsooth, to mate
    With those of such crude fashion, such great
        dearth!

'Tis even labor slight to dress up sin
    In guise of goodness, — "Families now too
        great!"
We hear (the dower too small), and, "Procreate
Those most unfit,"—poor way for "fit" to win
    The race of numbers,—and cut short debate.

Rome argued somewhat so, precisely, France,
    And lo, hurls down the irresistible Hun
    To prove once more to each new age begun,

By logic answerless of death's mischance,
  That war's god and the god of love are one.

His way with one or two is letting sin
  Work out its own results, in its own ways;
  And peace is good so long as peace obeys;
But war fulfils then virtue's discipline
  When o'er-ambitious greed 'gainst destiny
    plays.

With blazing eyes intense, indignant Life
  Cries out from every struggling living thing:
  " Who aids me, life eterne to him I bring;
But child disloyal in my awful strife
  Let Death him guerdon, Death he chose as
    king.

" My purpose clear runs past and onward through
  The form you have to-day, all form and phase;
  Think you that I who fill with life and raise
A million forms care aught for fatuous you,
  Who hug your paltry self some petty days?

" My peril greater with your danger grows,
  As fashion, polity, and law cement
  Self-seeking into system, government;
Crime multitudinous, rebellion shows,
  Whose answer is wild war's arbitrament.

" Incorporate guilt that hides, hides not from me
  And manifolded, grows not therefore less;
  Lusts institutionalized more clear confess
How fierce the purifying fire must be
  To burn out all the secret noisomeness.

" One sin there is that cannot be forgiven,
  All lesser wrong from this alone derives:
  Who with me works, for my plain purpose
    strives,
Need fear no fate; but never shall be shriven
  Disloyalty, while heaven or hell survives.

" All happiness is my warm gratitude;
  When pained my loyal child, from farthest sky
  I come to bring sweet sleep and justify.
Rewards innumerable wait, unguessed, renewed,
  My brave coworker, or my least ally.

" Then beauty, God's own smile, shall lighten, run,
   And break through all the world's face, shine
   With far-near loveliness, divine,
Like morning over sea, o'er land the sun,
   His love's triumphant blessing, seal, and sign !"

THE MOUNTAIN BROOK

Except the Master's will
You have no wish, no other pleasure know;
At slightest hint from Him you fall and go,
    Or wait, commands to fill.
(If thou, O heart, such wise obedience knew!)

    "Be pure!"—Each pool and nook
Transparent, limpid, still, invites one see
The far blue heaven it loves and mirrors free,—
    Ah, blessed, blessing brook!
(Wert thou, perturbèd soul, so frank and true!)

    "Be kind!"—To you, for drink,
Crowd roots of flower and tree; on confident
    wings
There flutter down sweet wild-eyed gracious
    things;
    In depths your fishes shrink.
(Thy loves and givings, soul, how poor, how few!)

" Be happy !"—Joyous, free,
Your ripples run with breezes, dance with light,
Down hurrying pebbles laugh, or, hiding flight,
    Gurgle away in glee.
(O heart, we once were little children too!)

" Must lose thy life !"—Countless
The drops for you renouncing self, and thence
Your beauty all, and your beneficence,—
    Yourself their fused caress.
(For all thy greed what gained the world anew?)

Through soiled, sad world of man
Leads down your destined way. Accept your
    fate!
And unto purifying sea translate
    All human wrong you can.
(Hast thou cleansed world as has one drop of
    dew?)

BLIND

WITH gliding, soft, caressing touch
  His fingers lingered long to find
Some hint of orchid-beauty. "Such
  May be," he sighed. My friend was blind!

"This flower is very God," I said
  To Beauty's priest, trained artist-mind;
He praised, but pitying shook his head;—
  This friend, I fear, was also blind!

AT THE PLAY

THE stage-play was not half so prized
   As drama that was played near by
By neighbors four—quick recognized
   Two lover-pairs, though wondered I
Why elder man chose younger maid,
And boyish fellow his court paid
   The girl whose years began to cry.

No matter! Who these days is fool
   Enough to doubt love's ways or art?
The poorest scholar in his school
   His lesson learns and knows *by heart;*
He questions not nor disobeys,
Sings or recites when teacher says,
   To young or old maid, sweet or tart.

'Twas clearly seen the little play
  " Full-dress rehearsal" was, leastwise
Suspected not the actors they
  Had audience of other eyes,
Deep interested in the plot—
The old, old way, but clean forgot
  By love, too happy to surmise.

The old way too of wily one
  Who watches sly the innocents,
And, seeming blind, sees all the fun—
  Thinks " what fools these !"—but longs, repents
The vanished day when he so acted,
When he, as they, was wild, distracted,
  With glorious love's improvidence.

The dear side-comedy of four
  Was pantomime,—best sort of play
For sense alert; though the *encore*
  Is oft demanded, yet obey
The gracious actors every time,
As if they loved themselves the mime
  More than whate'er spectator may.

The plot was deep and intricate,—
    Just what it was I need not tell
If I found out,—it's overlate
    To care now for the plot, when—well!
When th' acting is the one great thing
To make smiles, sighs, and tears upspring
    From hearts that age—and yet that swell!

Most perfect was the acting here,
    And exquisite beyond compare
In those great nothings that are near
    To everything, and make despair
The poor stage-mock,—the gesture, tone,
Nuance and hint, half hid, half shown,
    That captivate, bewitch, ensnare!

Each one, 'twas plain, felt deep his part,
    And acted as if real the play;
The cheek's soft flush came from the heart
    Of both the maids, so pleased were they
To have such perfect lovers,—not
Too much insistent, yet who caught
    Least hinted call to meet, convey

Deliciously ignored caresses;

    (Had they been noticed, quick repelled!)

Desirings masked in bashfulnesses;

    Deft make-believes, and doubts, soon quelled;

Tense little soft, half-slipped suggestions,

Remonstrances arousing questions—

    (Sneer not, old mumbler, late rebelled!)

The tell-tale flush in elder maid

    Less riant was, the eyes' bright gush

Not quite so artless, unafraid,

    As in the flowering bud the blush;

It smiled its victory more than laughed,

And drank its joy in long, slow draught,

    With reveried, inner, happy hush.

It seemed somehow as if she had

    Suggestion faint, a merest touch

Of mother-way for the dear lad,

    Unschooled in love—you know—just such

As we, old man, in truant days,

Felt kindly o'er us fondle, graze,

    When boy-love bothered *her*—not much!

But placid, calmly happy, she,
   In long-sought, sure-found blessedness
That fills all spaces full and free
   Of inlet, nook, and shore-recess,
With roll serene of mastering tide
That bathes, floods, drowns all, in its wide
   High, limpid, splendid lordliness.

The "bud" was like, yet different—
   She had (again similitude!)
The self-same sweet abandonment
   Once your own girl had (how subdued
She mopes beside you now!) when you
Her—years ago—much closer drew—
   (After the play, 'tis understood!)

Her eyes were luminous with delight;
   A little tremble quivered deep,
And Joy ran fluttering, half-affright,
   Back to her heart, where Love, asleep,
Lay nestled and awaiting time
When she should call, and he should chime
   And ring his bells in reckless sweep.

But she low-whispered him, " Not yet!
  Wait just a little longer, sweet!"
And, hovering o'er him, with regret
  And gladness mixed, she hushed, discreet,
The dreamer down,—" Not yet, dear king,
I give you leave to rouse and ring;
  Sleep now!   Soon come my hurrying feet!"

Her " escort" also had the air
  Of slight protectorship, a feint
Of father-right, submerged, as 'twere,
  Beneath the wooer's great constraint;
His dignity could not control
His tenderness, which peeped and stole
  Through eager smile and gesture quaint.

Indeed, the younger lover showed
  More plain his bolder consciousness
Of strong-armed duty that he owed
  His gracious gentle sorceress;
'Twas surely genuine, old-time love
That held so fondlingly her glove,
  But proud, too, in roused manliness.

Each with the other seemed to vie
    In pleasing most his chosen maid,—
A race of wish, and hand, and eye,
    To meet wish unexpressed, repaid
With grateful smile, or dainty tease,
Superfluous both, yet pleased to please—
    Such love's old merry masquerade!

No chance was lost of touching hand,—
    Quite needless, true, but recognized
By each as necessary,—and—
    'Twas noticed that, howe'er disguised,
There were sometimes long lingeringnesses,
Faint little squeezes, or impresses—
    Nay, once, I'm sure, hers sympathized!

One play was over—not the other:
    Adjusting wraps gave prized permission
Quick-granted, taken, again to smother
    Caresses five, without suspicion.
In passing down the aisle I heard
Ironic question, answered word,
    Revealing how I missed my mission.

'Twas elder man asked elder maid,—
    "What think you of the actor's part?
And did you better much by trade?
    You see I've won your daughter's heart!"—
"Your son, sir, is almost the beau
That you were twenty years ago,—
    But *you* played with too earnest art!"

And then her eyes began to water—
    "This trading years for youth is sweet,
But is too dangerous for our daughter;
    You surely were too indiscreet."
"I see," said he, "how matters run;
Hereafter I'll watch out my son
    Shall not with me for wife compete!"

HIS EXPLANATION

You beg me tell you how it came
  That I could do such foolish thing!
How could one be again the same?—
  I spoiled your dinner,—who could wring
  A smile (except in sleeve) or bring
To life again joy's watered flame?

Now when one makes himself an ass
  I know he should go far away
To eat his thistles or his grass,
  And farther still when he would bray,—
  But whom, dear madame, let me pray,
As much as me hurts my trespass?

Too plain indeed was the constrain
  I brought among your guests and laughter,
The kind ignoring of my pain,

The gay before, the forced thereafter,
  Looks fixed in plate or glance to rafter,—
The secret all concealed in vain.

You thought it safe, I thought so too,
  'Twas after these so many years—
Inviting me to dine with you,
    For who could have a hint of tears—
    One's sweetheart's husband kills such fears
And leastwise guests and children two!

But then men's hearts have strange diseases
  (*Your* health of us has little heed)
Old battle-scars a scratch displeases,
    Condition met they burst and bleed
    And tell the tale to them that read
Of old-time woe no time appeases.

You guess the rest, why need I maunder?
  Your head half-turned revealed that curl
Of which I once was witched and fonder
    Than—no matter!—what a whirl
    Again comes in my brain, dear girl,
As I upon that evening ponder.

Who would have thought 'twould grow once
    more
   That wild, sweet, wondrous, wicked skein,
Precisely as it was before,
   And like the one these years has lain
   Against my heart since that far vain
And maddened hour upon the shore?

To question, hint, assenting say,
   Whate'er you may, whate'er they will,
The blind (hearts too) must have their way,—
   But sob may gush and eyes o'erfill
   Despite all laughter and all will
If rise the ghost of buried day.

AFTERMATH

Down lover's lane well shaded o'er,
  Walked wife and I, as years
And many a happy year before
  We went, when love and tears
Came quicker and were easier swore
  Than now our tears and fears.

A couple half as young as we,
  Slow sauntering toward us came,—
Of two, at once knew secret, three,
  Her tell-tale glance and flame,
Concealing made more plain to see—
  Sweet proof of sweeter shame.

Ah, blissful face and furtive eye
  Of captive, conquering maid!
Sweet mix of pride and meekness shy,
  By hidden blush betrayed,

A hint of tears and many a sigh,
  Desiring yet afraid.

But bud will yearn to flower, His grace
  God writes in feature fair,
While prophecies with promise race,
  And eager to prepare,
Works happy love in form and face,
  In breast, and everywhere.

The meaning of that flush suffused
  By heart's soft palpitance,
Caught, half with scorn and half amused,
  The wifely eyes' mischance :—
"The jade ! her very lips accused
  Their kissed inheritance !"

"Dear girl,—my girl !" I laughed with glee,
  "Years, years ago, you had—"
(Those other two turned, hearing me)—
  "That selfsame look, egad,
When here, as now, I kissed you—see !—
  Angry again, yet glad !"

A FLIRTATION

Though past, sweetheart, it was, you know,
　　Such perfect sweet!
Like all delights, alas, 'twas, oh!
　　Too short and fleet!

Yet while the charm endured, we gave
　　Our best and all,
Disdained reserve, to hold, or save,
　　Whate'er befall.

And *con amore* played our parts
　　The old mad way,
Concealing well we risked our hearts
　　In reckless play;

And license gave the glorious hour
　　To wreck or rule,
While lasted "run" and "drawing power,"
　　Of our "Love's School."

We would not let suspicion rise
  To check or warn;
Our hearts (and lips!) were shrewd and wise
  To outwit scorn.

We knew that destiny would send
  Quite soon enough
And smooth would shape the drama's end,
  Or hew most rough!

We kept our consciousness well hid
  Like expert ones,
And in "rehearsal" we forbid
  All skips and shuns

Of "business," for so, we knew—
  At least sure, I!—
You'd better thus at your début
  Act, kiss, and sigh.

Your first rehearsal 'twas (my last?)
  Yet, 'pon my soul,
'Twas Cupid picked you out and cast
  You for the rôle.

Dear Ingenue, I trust that he
    Who'll take my part
On Life's great stage (passée, you see,
    Alas, my art!)

Will love as pure and warm (what!—Tears?)
    As I of late
With all my fifty gathered years
    Have loved your eight!

INTER ARMA LEGES SILENT

FOUR feet rest upon the fender,
  (Two are clumsy, two are neat);
Four eyes silent gaze and tender
  (Two are serious, two are sweet)
At the pictures in the fire,
Made of wishes, dreams, desire,
Burning ever rosier, higher.

One foot slips against another,
  (One insistent, one discreet);
One hand glides across to other,
  (Hands more foolish are than feet);
One chair draws the other nigher,
Brighter are the flames and higher,—
Is it not a dangerous fire?

Two feet now have left the fender,

    (Which two would you have supposed?)

Two eyes earnest fix two tender,

    (Two wide-open, two half-closed);

One hand firm another wedges,

One mouth protests while one pledges,—

Silent inter arma leges!

THE BACHELOR'S BALLADE

THE wife of neighbor number one
   Hath found her husband is a bore,
For books he careth, she for none;
   He readeth, writeth, evermore,
   While she receptions, teas, galore
Doth do,—and him she maketh go
   Sometimes, though he do swear, implore,—
For Life and Love will have it so!

The wife of neighbor two's undone,
   Her heart it acheth grievous sore
Because he to the club doth run,
   And doth society adore,
While she home stayeth, thinketh o'er
Her wrongs—" Neglected wife," you know,
   And all the rest oft heard before;—
And Life and Love will have it so!

What hath been done remaineth done,
  The law doth say.   But as I pore
It wondereth me why husband one
  Did not in courtship days afore
  The wife of number two adore,
And wife of one find proper beau ;
  If Life were wise and Love knew more,
Then Life and Love would have it so !

ENVOY

Be wise, O lovers, I implore,
  As wise as I to choose, and slow;
Full fifty years I've sought, or more,
  For Life and Love shan't have it *so !*

SATISFIED!

I'M satisfied, regardless aught
That fashion wills, or wills it not;
   Sweet eyes are sweet, or sweeter far,
   To serf than they can be to Czar,—
And Czar of serf may covet cot.

For ladies great tie true-love-knot
No more expert than maids whose dot
   And coat-of-arms their faces are;—
      I'm satisfied!

One bird in hand for two uncaught
Of sweetest singers in the grot
   Would be exchange upon a par
   With canvas-back for caviar,
Or rich Miss V. for girl I've got,—
      I'm satisfied!

THE LOST MATE

ALREADY far below the shadows gloamed,
  While still upon my mountain-home up there
The sun's gold rays yet shone, and, high o'er-
    domed,
    The sky flushed deep with luminous hues so
      fair
The startled heart stood rapt with subtle dreams
Of paradise, such pure, unearthly gleams
  Shot through the rose-empurpled sea of air.

The miracle of sunset so filled full my eyes
  I failed almost to note far down below
A lone brown bird from out the valley rise,
  And toward me wing with weary beat and
    slow;
He lighted near, and without wait for breath
Pealed out a throbbing cry that seemed of death
  Presageful, and of hopes that deathward go.

Full well from childhood I had known the bird;
  In all the yellowing fields and summers long
His call courageous, bright, and clear, had heard
    Commanding, "Up, Bob White!"—as, soft and
      strong,
The caressing shine and shadow of the sun
Chased o'er the ripening grain in waves that run
    Like love and laughter undulant along.

But this was not the old familiar cry;
  Although of notes the same, it had a clang
So different, so palpitant, and high,
    As if from heart half-breaking it outrang,
Stabbing the silence of the evening air,
Reverberant of desperate despair,—
    "My mate! oh, little mate! where art thou,
      where?"

Alas! To that alert and listening ear
  No answer came, and circling half around
The crest again, he stopped,—again I hear
    The unutterable pathos of that sound!

Once more half down the precipice, enthralled,

I caught it,—then no more, no more it called,—

That last lone cry of love in sorrow drowned.

Back to the nest again, dear little brother, go,

Empty of mother-breast, the eggs all cold!

Thy grief than mine less poignant is that so

Thou dost not understand my pain that's old,

Nor thine that's new; from thee is wisely kept

The knowledge, memory, we must fain accept,—

The while one fate and love us both enfold.

Thy hurt's enough: I would not have thee know

A hunter killed thy mate, and that returned,

As thou, twelve others to lone nests below;

Thy pain were sharper yet if thou hadst
learned

I cursed the man who brought them all to me,

Thy limp, dead sweetheart one, for me to see,

While calling thou with throat and heart that
burned.

We wingless ones our mates have also lost—
   The hunter Fate is merciless to all—
And sometimes, when too passion-torn and tossed,
   We wonder if the woes and wants that thrall
Are not the orphan's gifts we got at birth
From our dear, dying, widowed mother Earth,
   Who, wanting God's love, found life's sweet was
      gall.

By misery stung, from our lone valley dim,
   With weary-winged and long forefelt despair,
We send our souls to cry about the rim
   Of heaven answerless, our hungry prayer
Of endless and unsatisfied desire,
That burns in hidden heart with hidden fire,—
   Soon back they wing to homeless home of
      care!

Your wiser, better world, I trust, dear bird,
   Knows no example more unfortunate,
Who never answering-call of mate has heard,
   Who feels no grief grow lighter, pain abate.

Far better lot is his whose mate has died
Than his whom love has never sanctified,—
    Kissed lips may mourn, but curse not later
        fate.

Thy hurt's enough: I would not to thee show
    How pitiable are our wretched minds and ways,
How poisons in our pulses beat and flow,
    Mock all endeavor, eat and end our days.
Go mourn thy wasted summer, mourn thy mate,
Nor be of our strange griefs importunate,—
    Another love may come, and other Mays.

But not to us! We ease, perhaps, our pain,
    Disguise, but not forget it, in our work,
Refight old battles, not, we trust, in vain,
    And hope behind the mystery and the mirk
That God's will, free and full and final, brings
An answering of all the questionings
    Which now beneath our thought and dreaming
        lurk.

But not to us! To us but once comes love,
  And then escapes if welcome wait too long,—
True bird of Paradise, God's homing-dove,
  With wings of splendor and with throat of
    song,—
Home flies and leaves us, what we'd fain forget,
Only ourselves,—while infinite regret
  Broods in our hearts the memory and the
    wrong.

WOODS-SECRETS

Here rest! Nor vulgar eyes, nor echoing
   From our far garish world will reach us here;
Here only come the pure,—no note they bring
   Discordant of the harmony so clear
Of stillness, waters, leaves, and birds that sing,
And gladness at the heart of everything.

      •

Here Silence stealthy slips and softly glides
   Among the trees, with white wan hand to ear,
The heart pressed down whose noisy beating hides
   The words that seem to come from far and near,
In mystic murmur, subtle, sweet, profound,
As if the air were flowering into sound.

Rest here! The leaves make perfect our retreat;
   Their arches form a cool, green, mimic sky,
Through which the sun's bold glances cannot
       beat,
   Nor curious clouds peer in as they drift by.

Both sun and cloud are mad to know, I fear,
What strange mysterious thing is doing here.

What stupid things are these same clouds and
   sun!
 The other sky-folk, they of wing and song,
Attend their own affairs; the squirrels run,
 After a moment's glance, while low and long
The rustling leaves sursurant lisp and sigh,
To hide our secret from profaning eye.

The brook's our dearest friend, O sweet sweet-
   heart;
 She too has loved, and loves, and still will love
When we are gone and others play our part,
 Forgetting earth below or heaven above,
Forgetting other loves and lovers true,—
 Or false,—as now are reckless I and you.

The brook, your sister, knows the secret wise,
 And talks of it between her banks of moss
That almost overclose, as when your eyes
 Are brimmed with pleasure, fall the lids across;

Delight with rippling shivers hides remote
And little gasps and gurgles fill her throat.

Beyond, the streamlet widens, and there rests,
   A placid pool that upward strains to reach
The boughs and grasses which, at her behests,
   Bend down to catch across the tiny beach
The pouted profferings, love's thirst to slake
With lips that linger long in give and take.

And there the ribbon-grass has found the wooing
   Beyond resistance, and has fallen fair
Into his mistress' arms,—most dear undoing!—
   Renouncing earth with all its light and air,—
As sometimes, sweet, do men,—are they unwise?—
Forsaking worlds for one loved pair of eyes.

Drowned, but in bliss, far down the slumbrous
     green
   Cool depths it waves, in slow lithe monotone
Of dream, whose undulations roll serene
   Upon her pulses, coursing down the prone

Soft, sinuous limbs, whereon it lies and metes,
Its whole life answering each of her heart-beats.

Let fall and flow your hair, love, where it will,
    And let your head fall down upon my arm,—
I shall not heed the arbutus-buds that spill
    Their fragrance in my face, and seek to charm
My eyes from yours, as through your scattered
       hair
They spy,—a flower-framed face than flowers more
       fair.

Ah, love! there come great seasons in our
       lives
    When feeling finds our souls so small that
       they
Must burst with all the ache and strain, as drives
    Relentless in our being's homelike bay
The thunder of the ocean-mothered tide,
Whose conquering waters o'er all shore-lines
       ride.

And now we know the secret, full, entire,
  Beloved, the wonderful and mystic word
That subtly creeps, then runs, like soft sweet fire
  Through roots and buds, through veins of beast
    and bird:
'Tis *Spring!* God's breath, that in us His life
  starts,
And *Love!* God's secret, told in our two hearts.

MOTHERHOOD

In love's own old-time foolish fondling way
  From very plenitude of tenderness,
  Her fingers grace with idle soft caress
Whate'er they touch, and lingering they play,
  With dreams and hopes in rapt forgetfulness.

One link of that great chain she makes her life,
  Which binds the past and future into one,
  That besides cannot be, her e'er undone,
Which anchors from our shifting world of strife
  To spirit's timelessness and stable sun of sun.

For mothers are the mediators between
  Our world and heaven; they bring the beauty
    bright
  Of God amidst our sin and want of sight.
Their faces and their children's long the sheen
  Retain of His endowing consecrating light.

Ah, father, husband, nothing thou shalt see
  In heaven or earth, reveals as to her eyes
  God's very Self, when they an babe that lies.

New-born beside her, play the lambent, free,
  Warm lightings of her love's emprise.

No proofs of logic firm, than truth more sure,
  No summary of science, Bibles, creeds,
  No lesson of world-wisdom, hero's deeds,
Refute as do those limpid eyes and pure
  The atheists' unbelief,—one glance succeeds!

Two fathers, God and man, her lovers are,
  And naught of all their dual loves that flow,
  Their riches through her heartways wide and
    low
She keeps, e'en adds her own, saved from afar,
  Till, surfeited the babe sleeps long, and slow.

Who thus, as she, their wills subordinate
  Find, far beyond all understanding, peace,
  An end of striving, lessening pain's release,
While in their hearts the joy of conquered fate
  Shall nestle down and sleep till dreaming
    cease.

Effulgent glows the crimsoned living blood
    Of love's grail and of life's, leaps strong
    From mother-heart, through nursling's veins
        along,
A tide mysterious at ebbless flood—
    A grail in every household, righting wrong,

Recalling duties, hope's inspiritings,
    Still stronger making strong, still fairer fair,
    By simply what it is, and being there,
Makes fathers Josephs, mothers Marys, kings
    Bring gifts, and angel-songs fill all the air.

LA CRUCHE CASSÉE

Two things there are that make the whole world
    bright,
  That down to our poor earth draw heaven
    divine,
  That up to their pure heaven lift earth, that
    shine
In joy and woe alike with quenchless light,
And make all wrong less wrong, all right more
    right:—
  The child and mother;—in each face the sign
  Of God's soft seal is fresh; His love benign
Laughs in their hearts all day, broods there all
    night.

O little maid, thou interblended gleam
  Of child that was, of woman yet to be,
  Which sweetest is we know not of the three—
The hope, the memory, or the painted dream.
Thou only, Art, canst changeless keep the mild
Faint evanescence of the woman-child.

But thee of pulsing love and life, dear child,
    Not even Artist of the Living Clay
    Could keep from going thy predestined way,
The woman-bud from flowering unbeguiled
    To rose as perfect as the bud might pray.

If flower, alas, it must!   But I, I fain
    Would pray that God's immortalizing kiss
    Might hold the charm of thy unopened bliss
In bud for aye, from blooming keep the pain—
    For naught that blooms can pain and fading
        miss.

So strict the law that even Sacred Art,
    The gladsome and serene, life's pain reflects ;
    And I, too, catch in thy sweet face suspects
Of tears, on-coming griefs, perplexèd heart
    Awonder what strange thing it is dejects.

Like thee I question, too, all arguments,
    And marvel why from thee He does not keep
    All woe away, awaking or asleep,
Thy face the glass of joy's improvidence,
    Nor day find reason, night no cause to weep.

For thee, indeed, I cannot help but think,
　　Despite my will, as somehow not of us,
　　But as a dream of God miraculous,
Or statue He as Artist does not shrink
　　To fill with His life's breath, o'ergenerous,

And place it smiling here—or suffering—
　　Example of His craft and handiwork,
　　Of what His angels are where grief nor ill
Becloud, nor waiting sorrows come to bring
　　The disappointments that our days fulfil.

I see thee standing timid as shy bird
　　Upon the threshold of thy womanhood,
　　Uncertain if the doubtful coming good
May trusted be, or if thou wilt have erred
　　In singing more than life's soft, faint prelude.

I see thee also, fear and wonder-filled,
　　Pushed on the pathway of receding youth,
　　Thy tender eyes regretting still the ruth
Of all the girlhood joys thy heart have thrilled,
　　Presageful of the sadder joy of truth.

And I the pathos of their mute appeal
  Would answer with my hand enclasping thine,
  And back thy steps unto thy home divine,
And Father, leading, we would pray repeal
  Of banishment to earth and fate's design.

MIGRATION

THE migrant birds I loved, the hopes, the loves,
    Like time and life, for other lands take wing;
Pleasures and faiths, the thrushes and the doves,—
    Far off I hear them fly, and sing, and sing,

As on their way to summer lands they fly.
    Winter and age they leave with me behind;—
With strong, fleet wings why may not also I
    Follow away to climes more warm and kind?

The sun shines cold and lower burn the fires
    Of youth and trust, ambition, and delight;
Snow covers now the earth, as age desires,
    While disappointments crowd and joys take
        flight.

The songs of birds and those of my young heart
   Sound faint and ghostlike, die away, and sigh;
Their hushed adieu is soft,—I start,
   And listen, as if, O God, 'twere Thy good-bye.

The lids fall shut, the evanescent dream,
   Like nestling bird in distant tropic grove,
Broods silent, wistful,—till renascent seem
   Fond life and hope beneath the breast of love.

Sweet singers, lovers of His love and light,
   Shall I like you once more find hope and youth,
Where life's sweet springs shall be renewed and
      bright,
   The heart relearn to love, reflood with truth?

As spring is ever in the world somewhere,
   When buds break into flower, birds nest and
      sing,
May wintered lives not also find that there
   Is spring divine for souls,—if souls find wing?

DAY-DREAMS

Farther, purer, grows the sky,
  Wan and paler fades the sea,
    Dies to zephyr now the breeze,
    Listless hang the leaves of trees
And the clouds o'er where I lie,
  Dreaming present hopes that flee,
Past regrets that do not die.

Time is flying, day by day,
  Month by month glides into years,—
    Life we ever mourn or wait,
    Too soon coming or too late,
Shirking work and losing play,
  Feigning laughter, hiding tears,—
Just the old and weary way!

All the griefs that will persist,
   All the things I might have done,
      Stare with large, reproachful eyes,
      Mocking wisdom most unwise,
Proffer lips I might have kissed,
   Want I have for love unwon,
World I have for world I missed!

THE FENCE

BUILD quick, O farmer, a fence there for me!
Build it as old as one ever could be,—
One of those old-fashioned fences, you know,
Made out of rails, twisty, criss-cross—just so!—
One "staked and ridered," but dangley and
      weedy,
Moss-grown and tumble-down, patchy and seedy.
Build it from nowhere to nowhere,—say, here
From this lot-center down where disappear
Rushes and cat-tails and alders and brook
Off in the woods-edge with winding and crook.
Scatter big stones too, and where there's a tree
Let it wind round it, scraggly-like, free;
There where that old one blew down, run along,
Hit all the stumps sure, for they all belong
To a good fence—the poor rails like to squeeze
Close as they can to the old mother's knees.—
Thus 'mong the trees and the bushes and trunks,
Homes I'll make, run-places, for my chipmunks,
Holes for my woodchucks, nests for my birds,—
Glimpses for me of the world without words!

THE MEDIATOR

By chance, or accident divined,
   A little seed toward the sky
Was wafted by a gust of wind,
   And left on ledge of window high.
It found a chink where lone, uncheered,
   It waited the predestined hour,
When life's sweet miracle appeared
   Of root and growth, leaf, bud, and flower.

And then despair with death-intent
   To that long-closèd window came,—
The human o'er the flower-face bent
   And heard a soft low whisper— " Shame !"
Then straight despair to honor grew
   And wore, life-through, a daisy brave
Above a heart, as daisy, true,—
   And thousands now grow on his grave.

MY CRITIC

I READ my poem to a critic wise and kindly,
And truer none!—
Of how I loved, and how I gently, madly,
blindly
Had wooed and won!
My critic wept, and murmured low—"An echo,
clear,
Of long ago!"
And then between her kisses, said, "Your
father, dear,
Loved me just so!"

BABY

A SENSE of his far-coming,
  Faint perfumes sweet,
Inaudible fine humming,
  About him meet,

As if one caught the whirring
  Of unseen wings,
The whispering and conferring
  Of mystic things;

A feeling too of waiting
  Predestined hour,
Preparing and creating
  A strange new flower.

His glance is made of wonder,
  And half of fears,
As if behind or under
  Were waiting tears.

He looks with mixed surprises
    At these strange things,
Desires with doubt's surmises,
    Half-lifts of wings.

A teasing hint of laughter
    Eludes to smile,
Then mocks you hurrying after
    With solemn wile.

Most marvellous things are doing
    Right there in air!
Or mighty thoughts are brewing,—
    To judge from stare.

To music he may listen
    We cannot hear,
His eyes so strangely glisten,
    And persevere;

The little fingers clinging
    About yours curled
As if afraid of swinging
    Back out of world.

Surprising awkwardnesses,
  And aimless jerks,
Up-caught forgetfulnesses,
  Tell how brain works.

Through eyes of her who bore him
  Gleams love divine,
You see as she bends o'er him
  How God's eyes shine.

The mellowed marble's sweetness
  Of her breast
He drinks, till, with completeness
  He sinks to rest.

What building, then, and working,
  Goes on in sleep!
What mysteries are lurking!
  Preparings deep!

While God is happy weaving
  Hid mechanism,
For suffering and achieving
  Far crown or chrism.

She too has fond still dreamings
  Of future dim,
Hushed hopes and secret schemings,—
  All, all, for him!

" How proud will be the mother
  Of her boy-man!
And then—will she—that other?—
  What woman can?"

CRADLE CROONING

BEFORE you came my bosom's drouth,
  Within, without, yearned long and still,—
The empty breast sought for your mouth,
  The empty heart for you to fill.

And now you're here, dear heart and mouth,
  How deeper is my yearning still
To drain my bosom's wealth to drouth,
  With milk and love your breast to fill.

DOLL-PHILOSOPHY

I LOVE my dolly and then she loves me;
When she's not naughty she's good as can be;
When she is naughty I scold her, and then
Harder I love her, to make up again.

Over in China the babies have eyes
With curious corners, most wonderful wise;
They're so good always and nice that their queues
Grow down to their knees or their queer little
shoes.

African babies and dollies are black;
They have no clothes on their breast or their
back;
Their heels they kick up as high in the air,—
High as they want to and nobody care.

Have angels babies, and these babies dolls?
I'd like to climb up and peek o'er the walls
Mammas and babies and dollies to see,
Mary with Jesus—ah, would He love me?

MARRIAGE AND DIVORCE

Lucy said Walter, of all she had had,
Was the best husband,—he never was bad ;—
Promised to bring him right over to me,—
Try him I might for myself and then see !
She introduced him—and most stylishly ;
I said, " Good-morning, will you marry me ?"
He answered " Yes" by a nod of his head ;
Quick then I put him straight on to my sled,
Hauled him for wedding-trip all round the square ;
All of our neighbors made compliments rare !
When we came home Walter said he was tired,—
Something more added seeming much like "all-
    fired."
Slippers I got him and also his pipe,—
Business was awful these days ; and the type
Of the newspapers so bad really
He could not read a bit longer, not he !

Then I was frightened he might go away,
Off to the club, or else down to the play,—
Perhaps to Lucy!—and then I jumped up,
Made him some tea in my sweet china cup,
Sang him " Over the Garden-Wall, Ha, Ha!"
Told him he was the best, nicest papa
My dollies said they ever had had,—
Would not he love them ? Please not be so bad !—
That ended the matter ! Off he went quick
To Lucy again. I cried myself sick !

AT SUNSET

FLING wide the windows, nearer draw my bed,
That I may rest my head upon the window-sill;
And with the dying day now let me die.
If you have pity, kindness, leave me here
Alone, unwatched. 'Tis shame enough indeed
To live in others' eyes one's whole life through,—
But die! Why even brutes do this alone,
And they know naught of all this glorious thing,
These darkening splendors filling world and soul.
Let death and sunset work their will with me!

My Aimée call that I may give to her
And take love's old, unfailing good-night kiss.

Through rifts of shattered clouds shine shafts of
            light,—
The sun's last looks of love upon his world.
Throughout the day his pathway has been clear,

No thoughtless or impertinent cloud has dared
Before his face appear; but now, alas!
They press upon the hero dying, weak.
But even in death he will not brook contempt,
And with the last poor remnants of his power
He rives and breaks them, burns their edges white,
Bursts clefts and openings through them every-
      where
Through which glance far o'er land and sea and
      sky,
His love for all his sky and sea and land.

Dear god of light! 'Tis so with me, your child:
Throughout my morning, during noon that burned,
Down all the long, delicious afternoon,
This wondrous mechanism of thought and sense,
This friend and servant, lover and beloved,
Knew not of pleasure other than my will.
But now I must crush through its pressing cloud,
See past, not with its fast-obscuring eyes,
Without the cold benumbèd fingers feel,
And hear with ears not tuned to this hushed air.
Oh! there are colors in the soul-sky, pure

As ever found the cunning retina

In fjord Norwegian or in Orient sky;

The spirit too has ears to music tuned

Of air ethereal and more subtly soft

Than sleeping silence of the Alpine peak.

I walk with spirit feet on spirit earth

Touch ghostly hands with other hands than these.

The mountains are for gods to live on, free

From mortal need or care or company;

High hills the godlike man will love and know,

And when the sun goes down and life has end

A supernatural beauty lights him then,

The outer vision answering glow within

Until the world sublimed to beauty pure,

Incorporate and incommensurate,

Is met by spirit at the threshold wide

Of body-temple, passion-freed and passion-filled,

When God and matter lose themselves in one

Long-lingering nuptial thrill of blended kiss.

Poor slave was I of tyrants Time and Fate,

But I failed not to wrench from them at last

My " Calvary Hill," and there upon it death,
My drop of time lost in eternal sea.

Unerring, accurate, as Fate itself,
Cuts half the broad horizon-edge around,
The line of light that marks the limit set
Of sea and sky.   Above, the conquered clouds
Melt into deeper shades of blue and dark
And stand afar in mute and sombre awe.
Below, the shiver and the sheen sweep down
To shore-curve sheer and sharp, like drawbridge
        dropped
Straight o'er and down from brilliant Paradise,
Which seems to open and invite us come.
So iridescent glow the splendors there
That invitation meets our doubt and fear,
For braver, purer than is human heart
Must be the spirit that would dare such pass.

Far, far, and faint, to either side there stream
Revelant soft translucencies of light
In color robed, deep dreams of green and blue,
Revealing yet concealing azured blush

And glory of far-coming mysteries,
The splendid secrets of lit heaven beyond
Slow fusing, fading to the dark that gains.

Within the shore-line billowing valleys gloam,
And upward stretch to where I lie and wait,—
A height wide-braced and buttressed by long
    slopes
Of rolling foot-hills where the cattle feed,
While dark still lines of living shades between
Mark where the brooks fall down to seek
Their mother sea, the loving and beloved,
Surrounded by their friends the forest trees.

Oh, I have hoped and feared and waited this
Large kiss of sun that now has come!
I knew you would break through that broken
    cloud
And o'er me your last benediction shed.
I bare my breast, turn face, wide open eyes
For you to burn your images in their depths,
Whence deeper as these pierce into the brain
I watch refine to spirit, blend and fade

Through scarlet crude, on, on through all the
    scale
To soul's own deepening blue, life's purpled
    death,—
Your message, Sun, has reached my spirit's soul!

If I this color-music could but follow on
And see-hear all its harmonies and chromes
That subtly sing their silences above
The noise of even our finest tones and tints!
To feel direct what now we cannot feel,
The infinite overtones and octaved hues
Of music in the immaterial world!

A whirring flash of shadow past me shoots,
With certainty divine of confident wing,—
A tuft of feathered sunshine or of thought—
Were I that bird, instead,—instead of this!
The humming-bird, perhaps, is God's own glance,
Enfleshed, and winged, on round to see, per-
    chance,
If any flower more perfect may be made.
Once came one close before my face, stood still

With wondrous wing-beat, peered into my eyes
With eyes that stung me with their piercing jet;
Strange luminous gleams of weird unearthly tints
Refulgent quivered, flashed about its head:
From that revelatory instant I knew God!—
I knew what He could do, would like to do,
And in some ransomed world has done I hope,
Where matter's obstinate crudeness does not bind
As here to fatal indirectness, want,
And pathos of our all-imperfect life.

As any, once I had the springing foot,
The eye infallible, and leg, and arm
That dared and held command of circumstance.
What joy in life and doing then! What pride
Of muscle answering mind, of conquering will!
Alas! the loyal hand is trembling now
Lest it may fail in brushing off the tears
Self-pity springs in disobedient eyes.

It seems but only yesterday, not years,
When baring head and breast to catch the breeze
I ran exulting o'er the wind-swept hills;

With bending trees I laughed, and billowing
  grass;
I shivered with the whispering of the leaves,
And held my breath to hear the silken, soft,
Sweet murmured hush of stately far-off pines.

The sun now touches the horizon-line;
The clouds stand far and silently regret;
The mystic light-path down to shore is gone,
And in its place a fine translucent blue,—
A phosphorescent memory and a dream.
To north and south green fades to nothingness,
And deeper fall the shadows in the woods.

In health we cannot stare at perfect form,
Full-filled with perfect life, unflinchingly,
Nor at the midday sun, unblinded, straight;
Both life and light, the world's two things divine,
At incarnation-plenitude, permit
No mortal eye of mind or sense to see
Effulgence more than mortal of their face.
Wherever Life works out her mysteries
She hides herself from curious gaze o'er-bold;

Her nude Shekinahs blindness strike in them
Who are not priests of Love, and hence of God.
O'er libertine and life-deriding scientist
His curses laugh in bitterest mockery,
Who through the barriers crush of modesty
And reverence about all things divine.
To call that love or knowledge, what these get!
'Tis piteous that we cannot pity them!

Ah, child, I did not know that you were here
Until—your way—I found your little hand—
Just like your mother's—slipped between my two.
And I was maundering bitter stuff, untrue,
With my poor head, because—perhaps because
You did not come to keep me true and good.
My darling one, in all the coming years—
You   need   not   let   him   know   you   know   it,
          though—
And whether life bring joy or still more tears,
Forget   not   that,   however   strong,   however
          wrong,
Still, still, man's strength and power come clear
          from you,

His wrong because to this you were untrue.

You're young, I know, to tell of such old things,

But tears have pushed your budding plant

Of life to hurried flower; besides,—weep not—

I must go far and leave you here alone.

Oh, did I say alone? Ah, no, no, no!

Dear God has wrought a million years for you,

Their summers all are melted in your spring;

The bloom of all their fruits is flushing soft

Beneath your cheeks and lips and skin. The sun

Did surely weave your hair, and in your eyes

I see the mysteries of the stars and skies.

First with your hand and then more sure with
       lips

You close my mouth, as if to say, *Say not!*

My brain I know is fevered, but works true

In what I would have said. Or what or who

Hath made you out of sunshine, years, and tears,

Compacted resume of myriad hopes and fears,—

And His the grief and joy as well as ours,—

Will guard you still and guide you on, most sure,

Thou gladsome essence of a thousand loves

That lit the world's dark ages past,—not so!—
I mean 'twas only one love filling all,
Life's chiefest instrument—nay, very Self!

Good-night, my child, I'm overtired, would sleep—
Good-night! Again? Good-night!—And—now
   —good-night!

NOTHING—EVERYTHING

The sun thy playmate be, and stars thy nurse!
  Fill full thy heart with every day's sunrise,
  Thy blood recrimson with the sunset dyes;
Drink hill-top winds, with brooks and woods con-
      verse,
And all wild living things with love coerce.—
  In some still hour, before thy startled eyes
  Will then, serene and sweet, Truth smiling rise,
Life's riddle read, make friend the universe!

No other way! With hungry eyes and sad
  Philosophy and Science confess defeat,
    Crawl disappointed from their graves and fling

Their *Nothing* down,[5] while swell the bird-songs
  glad,
And over graves, in hearts and harvests
  sweet,
And everywhere, Love write his *Everything*.

(*A song is heard from the next room.*)

THE MESSAGE

From tropic land where day was long,
  Where sun was warm and life was sweet,
A tiny seed by some strange wrong
  Was brought to clime where cold and fleet
Were days and sun, and life and song.

It grew, for grow it must and would,
  Though bitterer was each growing hour,
Misdoubting, mocked, misunderstood,
  In pain it wrought exotic flower,
For flower brings love, and love, life's good.

One day with eyes of humming-bird
    God looked in on it, stopped, and low
He whispered some soft wondrous word,
    And flying south, cried out, *You know!*
And nodded south the flower—*I heard!*

(*After a silence, the voice again sings.*)

GIVE LOVE THY ALL

Love will find thee and will bind thee,—
    Follow thou his feet!
He will chasten and will hasten
    Bitter days and sweet;
Ripening sorrows, hurrying morrows,
    Life so slow, so fleet.

Give him thy all, beyond recall,
    Cherished, utter last!
Soon back to thee like tide of sea,
    Filling, thrilling, vast,
Will come thy love, with God's above,
    Hold thee ever fast!

My child who sings my songs to comfort me!
I'll ask her mother, she who sang them first,
To sing them there for me, or we'll come here
And hand in hand we'll hear the orphan sing.

Like stare of dying man grows stern the sun;
Resentful of our gaze, controlling fate,
He hurries on to death, sinks rapid down,
With steady eye unconquered and unclosed.
Then, like the deeds and life of a good man
Illuminating world that he has left,
Glows all the regions of the vanished orb
With reflex of the light it knows no more.

I follow soon, but till the darkness come
I hold my eyes and heart full to their work!

I cannot see the East, but well I know
Already flushes there each roseate hue
The eye can revel in, tongue not describe;
From orient to zenith deep suffused
The pale cloud-depths are vision, memory-filled;
They tell the mystery of his morning-love,

The dazzling splendor of his glorious noon,
The after-lights of his long afternoon.

That love-revealing, love-concealing blush
Arouses recollection of the day
When o'er me swept, high over me, and through
The wondrous passion-flood of wild sweet woe
That reckless fills, and drowns, and overfills
Our farthest waiting bays and thirsting shores,
With might of ocean's irresistless tide.

ONCE MORE!

Within her home of heart Song lingers still,
　　And begs for voice her longing to relate;
　　But palsied age is inarticulate,
And reminiscent of the old-time skill,
Song sits adreaming of the riant will,
　　Of days when love was sweet and passionate,
　　When flower, and bird, and beauty, warned too
　　　　late
That day was passing and that Death would kill.

Once more, O Life, let pulses throb and flood
  With recklessness and eager hungry blood!
Once more, O Love, give back the dear torments,
  Desire insatiate, the tender, wild
Firm cling of mouth to mouth,—th' omnipotence
  Of life, by world, nor time, nor fate beguiled!

The hour slipped past, as glides the life away—
The offered *once* is quick replaced by *never*,
If indecision fail to grasp and hold;
Then time becomes a vanishing regret,
And grows regret to bitter lesson's pain—
As once I wrote ere yet I knew how true
The words, how near I was to know them so!

THE WORD OF LIFE

When Life was set the task of making here
  A home for God,
He whispered one great word into Her ear,
  With warning nod.

This word Life puts at heart of whate'er breathes—
    Her death parole,
To grass and tree, to beast and man bequeathes
    Their virtue sole.

'Tis this command that makes each tiny cell
    Our unknown slave;
Let one of all the millions once rebel,
    We find our grave!

'Tis known of no ascetic, wounded, sore,
    Stifling his breath,
But only by the loyal who ignore
    Or hate all death.

Obedience to it makes all truths and rights,
    Makes evil good,
And disobedience is the sin that blights
    All brotherhood.

By thousand words men seek to say this word,
    But all are vain;
'Tis lived and loved and felt, by no ear heard,
    No science fain.

'Tis *Love* and *Live, Know, Forward,* and *Endure !*—
    Than these far more !—
'Tis heroism, coward-scorning, pure
    Deep science-lore.

The hint of it is caught in silent night
    When heart-beat wakes,
In eyes of child hides shy and sweet its light,
    In mothers', breaks ;

In healing wounds of flesh and tree, in surgeon's
    knife,
    In battle cry—
Auvergne, here ! And *Drink thy blood !*[6]—'tis life
    Of Beauty's eye.

It quivers passion-fired the nerves along
    In love and hate,
Burns sharp in pain and prayer, sings poet's song,
    Binds mate to mate.

The mystic word of Life, which no one saith,
    Which in all glows,
Learns each, one moment after earnèd death,—
    None other knows !

(After a pause Aimée again sings from the next room.)

THE CONSOLATION

When sun goes down and night is nearing,
When no more fears are left for fearing,
  When world fades out and time is flying,
  And no more tears remain for crying,—
    What comfort then has heart that dies?

When Love refuses more endearing,
And ghosts of dead hopes bring no cheering,
  When weariness is tired of trying,
  And Fate has even ceased denying,—
    What use has then or truth or lies?

Ah, death is opened heaven nearing,
And self that dies is life appearing;
  The truth is mind's sure deifying,
  Sweet love is God's sweet prophesying,
    And sunset here is there sunrise!

Up from the dewy darkening woods below
Floats clear the thrush's limpid good-night song,—
Ah, no!   'Tis bird that sings, the song is God's!
Dear Father, they who think Thee solemn, far,
Know not Thy birds, Thy children, gladsome,
        free
And filled with Thine own tenderness and glee.

(*Again the voice, as before.*)

GOOD-NIGHT

Good-night, dear bird, and warm beneath thy
        wing
            Thy nestlings keep,
Till morning come with light and song to bring
            An end of sleep.

Good-night, dear day, the twilight 'neath night's
        wing
            Nestles to sleep,
And stars will watch till sun shall morning bring
            From orient deep.

Good-night, dear world, beneath life's infinite
    wing
        I softly creep,
Till earth to heaven morn, and ending bring
        Of death's sweet sleep.

The song to silence trembled; soft and slow
The twilight hush stilled down to hush of night,
Then noiseless steps approached, the door ajar
Was held, and forward leaned a pale, sad face
That seemed a child's and yet a woman's too,
So sweetly poised was life between them both :—
"Asleep, dear father?   Shall I bring a light?"

NOTES

1. Page 30. By travellers the zoologic fact upon which this sonnet is founded is said to occur somewhat frequently in the Norwegian and Swedish lakes. The fact is as old as the *Mabinogion,* in which the eagle Gwern Abwy answered Gwrhyr, "And when I came there I struck my talons into a salmon, thinking he would serve me as food for a long time. But he drew me into the deep, and I was scarcely able to escape from him." P. 247.

2. Page 35. It seems unnecessary to refer to the incomprehensible string of figures given by physiographers of the estimated number of tons of solid material brought to the ocean by the rivers.

3. Page 66. These verses are a paraphrase of the next, entitled *Contemplation.*

4. Page 69. See note 3.

5. Page 152. The allusion is to the famous tomb and inscription, in which a figure is represented as crawling from the grave and scrawling upon the side the word *Nada*—"Nothing."

6. Page 158. "In the autumn of 1760, Louis XV. sent an army into Germany. The Marquis de Castries despatched a force of twenty-five thousand men toward Rheinberg. They took up

a strong position at Klostercamp. On the night of the 15th of October, a young officer, Chevalier d'Assas, was sent to reconnoitre, and advanced alone in the wood at some little distance from his men. He suddenly found himself surrounded by a number of the enemies' soldiers. Their bayonets pricked his breast, while a voice whispered in his ear, "Make but the slightest noise and you are a dead man!" In a moment he understood the situation. The enemy were advancing to surprise the French camp. He called out as loud as his voice could convey the words, "Here, Auvergne! Here are the enemy!" The words decided his fate. He was at once cut down. But his death had saved the army. The surprise failed, and the enemy retreated."

The battle-cry of Roland: "Drink thy blood, Beaumanoir, and quench thy thirst!"

www.ingramcontent.com/pod-product-compliance
Lightning Source LLC
Chambersburg PA
CBHW020550270326
41927CB00006B/787